STELLA VINITCHI RADULESCU

my dream has red fingers

Pittsburgh, PA

ISBN 1-58501-050-2

Request for information should be addressed to:

CeShore Publishing Company
The Sterling Building
440 Friday Road
Pittsburgh, PA 15209
www.ceshore.com

Cover design: Michelle Vennare - SterlingHouse Publisher
Typesetting: McBeth Typesetting and Design
CeShore is an imprint of SterlingHouse Publisher, Inc.

Printed in Canada

Acknowledgments:

The poems "simple touch" and "dear mother" appeared in
PLEIADES (Central Missouri State University)

"Why - do they shut Me out of Heaven?
    Did I sing - too loud?"

                                    Emily Dickinson

CONTENTS

PEACE COMES like SNOW

TIME TO RUSH

to finish the poem
unless you are dead -
dead just like me   stiffened
stretched out on top
of the page -
a strange constellation
of immaculate bones
and dreary flesh

dead like the one inside me
next to me   listening
to the old chapel growing
around:
bells vaults and columns taking
their shape
skies and trees loosing
their heights

rush rush
to finish the line you never
started never went
so far -
never measured the size
of your grave
with dark consonants
and flying sounds

when my words
were in prison I used
to see them every week at least
two or three times
bribe the guards or simply
break the wall
with my teeth:

extremely cold rough were
the vowels - children of hunger
and loss -
someone said something about
a party going on
in the world

I can't remember how long
lasted the winter
I had the mouth and the throat
already full of snow
today
I am still shoveling
the roads
I am still tapering the walls
with my lips
waiting for those words
to be set free

sometimes I find blood
on my handkerchief
and I think
this is how we are awaken
from a long long
sleep

EVERY day's chill

and the love I was longing for
brought me to this big
skeletal city
neither heaven nor hell -
however angels are taking sometimes
their turn in my dreams
and devils my silence
as granted

I have learned to forget
and to fail
I have learned to walk on empty
unfriendly streets
to talk
to say hello to strangers

I have met names and names
floating without bodies along
the lake
stones
unfinished lists like those
in Saint Luke's Cemetery

I have experienced the spring
without your violet- bluish
eyes and the smell of forsythia
but most of all
I have learned how to carry to keep
under my tongue
a small sound - a bead -
with the sour strong taste
of the yeast
my mother used to melt with
her hands in our daily bread

wHERE

from here? I know you like unanswered
questions
you know I like soft places under the sun -
for the sake of our unborn dreams
let's say something
let's say something to the world
fill the air with tiny
fluffy words
so we both could be imagined as such:
half human half sound

could find a decent place
to sleep
not far from the sea
not too close
to our last house

MORNING SNOW

an early whisper in my ear -
tears and joy will come later
when my mother comes home
again
with our daily bread
and two bottles of milk
in her hands
when the smell of milk
fills up the world
like her body: a blossom
of snow
an explosion
of flowers

MY TRUTH IS BEHIND THOSE DOORS

where we used to live
and to die
intoxicated by our own movements
and thoughts -
fear and smoke
too much smoke   no one could ever
take a deep breath
or a walk by the sea -
the Black Sea   where
one day I discovered a woman
buried in waves   with long long
green legs
dark starry hair and
my own face

what is

now in your hands: another hand
a tiny hand of a child a tiny
bird waiting to be released
up up in the sky

what is
here
inevitably tender white
rising or falling apart
ready to be concealed framed
in your heart -
a picture   black and white
next to your bed:

what is
dark gets faster into your blood
what is meaningless
tells you again and again the story
of our lives and death

what is
memory is over   let me put away
that piece of junk
far far in the invisible yard -
stars will take care of it
and start tomorrow
a new language

THE PIANO LESSON

forte fortissimo -
we are about to walk   to find
the river
to wash in joy and shadows our feet
we are about to arrive
to conquer the hour
to become trees

forte fortissimo -
and then sostenuto - the silence
like a beast swalows the light
coming through the rear window
tramples here and there
the remains
of our gestures

and the dark emerges from
each of us
as we stop listening or moving
in disbelief our lips:
quick quick   catch the wind
one more ride
one more sound

piano pianissimo - the smoke
of an old dream
and the stars bringing the sky
in our hands:
piano pianissimo: let us go
with the clouds

without end
without end

PEACE COMES LIKE SNOW

from the heaviest clouds
traveling west traveling
north
foreseeing the storm -
new memory   a new song
approaching the soul

are we the end or
the beginning
of life?

what is white and light
will touch again
our hands

exploring the sea

almost invisible

we are here don't say no I can
prove your presence by touching
the empty chair made of solid oak
and souvenirs
we are here I tell you look how
big our eyes -
and how many many arms hands
fingers
how childish how beautiful the earth -
today when spring takes over
and shovels the corpses
and the mother takes her baby
for a walk leans on my chest
to pick up
a tiny almost invisible flower

simple touch

       loving   everything at one time
       simple touch   one night   dust
       of years upon the earth
       golden sand

       isn't that me   my image
       over there
       coming out from the mirror
       growing around
       pushing with sharp rays
       the hours the air?

       isn't my breath the spider
       over there
       weaving my presence thread
       by thread:
       a painful burning wing
       which rises from the glass
       and fastens
       on my shoulders
       made of ice?

in absence

what I see from my window
is already a dream -
the rain drips from the roof
with no sounds for my ears

still trying to touch
the purple light behind
the tree -
but my fingers are no longer
here

eyes   poor eyes ready
to cry:
someone else gets
all the tears

call this day

he is here
his eyes next to my bed
in my fingers his truth -
so I can touch everything
with full confidence
as if I were the light
of the bright
afternoon

he is here
one step to the hill -
the rumor
the rush of the earth
the man
the cathedral   steeple after
steeple
building the sky:

call this day our child
our lonely child
begging for the seconds
to come

and we are walking on rocks
blue musical rocks trying to find
the end -
your hair burning like timber
your bones sparkling on the road
all the way to the sea:
one skeleton here on the edge
of the day
your twin above
in the sky

should we meet half way?
between? within?

the birds already went to sleep
cold -
there is no summer
in the ethereal tree -
no need
no sign of where
we haven't been

and you are here in my eyes
tempted to die
raising your arms your white
branches again
surviving
slowly eroding the sun

wild bushes

forgive me for having
entangled
your words
wild bushes
twisted
branches
narrow
doors -
forgive me for having
crowned you
with thorns

things change   winter
is gone
infested again with time
new stars
pulse at my wrists

you might whisper my name
at dawn
and think it's the wind -
nothing
nothing to be retrieved
from the last season from
the last night

new holes on the ground -
I am moving slowly
with all of our dead
with the seeds
towards new colors
towards the green

you might hear
the toll up on the hill
and think it's my heart:
so little
so little left
to celebrate
the spring

ALTERNATIVE

and if I had to choose
a place
a softer place to sleep
I would prefer the grass
which from your steps
keeps nothing but the silk

and if I had to choose
a time
a lighter time to be
I would be going
down the sun
where tides keep growing
as we grow:
an unpredicted dream

as for the soul -
I would prefer the tree
which from your coldness
your ongoing death
keeps nothing but the glow

INTERMEZZO

what are you looking for
in this park full of children:
wondering eyes   blue black
golden beads on the rope
of sun?

your childhood is gone -
playing with seconds
building a town
out of the movement
out of the sand happens
to be only the past only
what in the infinite space
doesn't have
any consistence or shape

like these small chimerical
hands
moving your silence
from stone
          to stone

exploring the sea
I found you
at the bottom
moving through ages
like an antique
vase
your shoulders
deep in the sand
where
there is no sign
of forgiveness -
your eyes filled with
stillness
and the stars
the little hungry
stars
devouring your
seconds
like worms

poetry I

dream
    of the earth
void
    of my voice
how painful
    to build
the silence
    within
a burning tongue

poetry II

too angel
to be able to fly
the horizon the stars
won't fit in your ethereal
eyes

too human
with all your arms
legs
and your big heart:

something between -
a warning for urgency
for a daily failure
something like
a blue faded light
in your yard -
a blue death
of both angels and
humans

will take you right
to the sky

poetry III

one and one
getting closer
to wisdom -
        wisdom
of my hands when
full of leaves
        waves
sleeping birds
they are able
        to touch
the emptiness
        of the day

o, yellow birds

be in time
you'll find me again
among lost things
and things
to come

be there
when I'll wake up
o, yellow birds
of your eyes!

dust and bones -
forget the light
petals again
from your breath

be ready
cover me

I am here
unborn   still
crucified

bleak eye

      eyes   ice
            flashing parts of the brain -
the others still sleeping
unfinished like rain -
           sleeping in my arms:
                      you
           made out of words
           made out of despair
                     ice
eyes again :
           given to the earth
           a gift for his time
are we ready to be here
alive
but cripple with only two eyes
           for all the shadows
           the flowers
           the trees
           for our whole eternity
                     eyes
eyes   ice again
bleak hour   as we dream   spring
after spring the flesh is getting
wings -
are we ready to be here
                    now
to be remember as such
are we ready to kill
                    our love?

THE MOTHER TONGUE

for Alexander and Nicholas

give me your hand said the mother -
the little prince walked closer to her
his minuscule hand   a leaf warm yet
fresh on a branch on a tree with big
miraculous eyes
the earth stopped grumbling and humming
the music of the mother tongue grew higher
and deeper from the sky to the ground soft
waves of vowels evening stars little white
shells pink tambourines and many many
names of cozy towns and wild
flowers -
give me your hand said
the mother again
and she walked faster
and she was scared -
strange names
were crossing the road like worms after a heavy rain
male names with iron glasses and plastic hair
Flack Knock Sword Culpepper names with teeth and
hooks dry consonants crumbling around the neck
they plick and plush they whip
and wrap they tense and tear
they bite
the ineffable light of the mother tongue -
give me your hand said the mother -
small sounds of despair were puzzling
the early birds all around the little
prince walked closer and closer to her:
he had two tears   one on each cheek
and a sudden dark fell on the road
(it happened yesterday it happens now and maybe tomorrow
again in Tennessee Virginia Spoon River Lauderdale in a
small town called Anywhere)

O, THE ETERNAL CORPSE

my dream has red fingers

my dream has red fingers
and walks on the streets -
guess whose legs
he is wearing
today

first
it was the snow
then
the blue boots
vanished

it looks like a mirror
bending my spine
folding the view
absorbing the sounds

careful   don't don't
step on my lips -
the silence
is your next stop

little by little I am moving
forward:
a small schooner
towards the shore
unfolding your hours
one by one

climbing from darkness heavy
roots   from a swamp
to the transparency
of your eyes
stealing the words from
everyone's mouth
hide stock them in all
the corners and cracks

to enhance your day
to enlarge your night
to choose the sounds of your
voice   the colors
of love

but your sleep goes on and on
it's so hard
to say
nothing

begging the rainbow

from my window
black and red fingers pointed
to my heart:
invisible you
like a piece of bread
in the dream of a hungry
child

always you
coming and going away
as everything one can say
as everything one can touch
always so: begging the rainbow
from a cripple sun.

dear mother

still snowing purple winter eyes
my blood keeps wiring the time
violins of rage on each window
each grave none of my souls
is willing to arise

still snowing purple winter eyes
my words keep digging the silence
at the bottom no wrinkles no tears
perfect world drawn into its own
blood

but one day one day I won my life
from you from this dark: stop crying
now in my flesh stop dying in my
hands dear, dear mother

o, the eternal corpse

it could be night it could be red
something near
or the Waste Land
the dust of the empty chair
or maybe more

maybe I could walk and walk
and go around
heart after heart from and for
the blasting scar

it could be even someone here -
just like me
on his way to resurrection
or to sleep

daily sun   daily hands   walls
lightning   tears

o, the eternal corpse who comes
to take his turn
in my dreams

the legacy of the body

                        it's about sound
about bubbling trees
and barking nights
                dripping days
                and neighing clouds
                it's about one word
                with thousands of heads
        growing and growing
around

and then about fear in a hot afternoon
                you and I
                stepping aside the lagoon
                where the sun
used to hold us a second or two;
                look down:
        the gold   the bottom
                is gone

time for sorrow and time
        for blindness
                for dead fiddlers
                        and dead dancers
time to endure the lack of time:
        the legacy of the body
                turning
                        to ashes

the metaphysics of love
starts here
with a tiny movement
a shiver between two blades
of grass
nothing

but the sound of a wound
angel or snake
something like an old music
coming out
from the ground
why

should I cry in the twilight
and rush into the dark
tears
turn to a new light
to a new question:
a small

talk on my lips
        healing
                the time

I didn't hear my father telling me
before he died: go, go ahead with your life -
although since then his words
traveled miles and miles
shivering at times   disappearing
fighting for life
no   I didn't hear them   that whisper
is here   unanswered   a stubborn bee
in my ear

no
I can not move my legs from the chair
next to his bed   move inch by inch
the time
all those heavy years -
waltzing swallows tear apart the sky
shattering over and over
the same little window - August -
August is terribly deep   high
deep and high like a well

no
not yet   I didn't crash his cigarette -
the smoke still gets in my eyes -
I hold with one hand the ashtray
and with the other thousands of stars -
small bodies
leaning on the edge of the time: no
between then and now I never
never crossed the line

by a rainy day

coming from nowhere
to this soft light to these
hands to these five fingers
jumping from nothing
to this breath to this dust
climbing from silence
to my voice
by a rainy day rainy world
rainy love:
now I can hear the music
that tune
which makes the grass grow

iNTERFERENCE

my feet hurt
bandages on both eyes -
to move on earth it's not easy
not easy at all
with all these bumps and dumps
sewers and spies
sleeping beauties and fallen
stars: right on your way
to the sky
- vivre dangeureusement -
don't swim too far little girl
don't swim too deep -
as you know
I was trained by the sea:
now
you can put new memories
new words
around my neck you can
burn my skin you can
open my chest - I have learned
intimacy
from the moon
nudity
from your name left on an empty
beach
     like
        a
           dead
              bird

here comes the day   a crown
of light -
love for the poor
from an unseen
God

the leaves of your absence
wake up
one by one -
here comes my blood   a crown
of fire -
love for the blinds

praying

alone
with my two hands -
praying
will stone
the air

alone
with my own heart -
dying
will kill
the night

THE BLUE SALAMANDER

> "Une salamandre fuit sur le mur. Sa douce tête d'homme répand la mort de l'été."
>
> *Yves Bonnefoy*

landing where

landing where nobody
landed before -
on a red hot spot   let's
call it our heart -
surrounded by water
deep water with the deep
taste of our past

look!   something slowly
opens blue wings
and moves and moves
toward us: it could be
the hour
the unexpected hour
we have just passed

suddenly alive

day night day
night
riding
the invisible
horse:
suddenly
alive

oNLy Now

only Here tells me
the truth
about living
a voice
a hole
between ashes
and hope

only Now tells me
the story
of an earth as blue
as the sea
lasting for ever
like you and
like me

only Never -
look! - sits
in our hands
and dies
like a flower

a cozy biRd

come to my house -
a cozy bird
will take your wintry steps
to build his nest

the dust of summer - easy
wings -
your life as granted -
time stands still

old love

sun of the dead
hatred of time -
reading the body:
a legend about an old
land about an old sea

beyond wisdom
a flower - breeze
of the last existing
thing

AGAINST MY VOICE

no   you are not my voice -
you are my child made out
of many many nights
of clouds and snow
and spherical bodies

no you are not my house
you are not my grave
that simple sound:
a knife
cutting into small pieces
my throat

no you are not my voice -
you are my child
the child I lost
o, loneliness
my growing lump
exploding everywhere
in the air

his mouth
waiting for the word -
the only word which could save him
take him down the road -

where we are praying
where we are bleeding
where thousand of silent fingers
are braiding the music -
the rope
to the next minute
to his next home

2

like a dream
like a cloud in a dream
a whisper   maple trees
vanishing at dawn

far away someone is writing
a love poem -
what I can do about it equals
the clumsy day

the blue salamander
tickling my hair -
here you are   your cold
unbearable tongue -
don't rush you said
don't rush -
it takes a life
to die

ANd

and
to continue it takes
the first step
the beginning of your
sentence
the first
letter
of
your first
word
and
the never
said
brought
to light
son
of your future
tongue

SONG

midnight -
the sun
in seclusion
shaping my body
in the form
of a swan

NEW STORIES ABOUT NOTHINGNESS

almost here   almost alive
stitches traps and flying leaves -
then the snow -
open the window   someone
must have left a sign for you
on the road
a stranger -
feel his absence   wait
for the wound - no breeze
no space
no time
there is one more winter
to come
and the streets
go on

history

my language grew wild
indeed
between bushes and weeds
personal hits all kind
flies and bees
typewritten swallowed
with tea
harlequins and clowns
went to the top
like clouds

one more angel
indeed
could even make history
climb the roof
the tongue
the grave -
bring to extinction
this day

but tomorrow

Now is already gone
but tomorrow is still
here:
cozy warm under my
pillow -
like an amoeba
like a fish
flapping and flapping
his timeless
wings

out of sight

beyond the surface
memories: the earth as such
corpse next to corpse
eye next to eye
feelings moving as slow as
under the water

jumping like a fish
a sudden joy:
unshapable desire to be
nothing   to be God -
I recall the sky moving as quick
as the time   then
the stream of a single day
carried everything
out of sight

to arrive at the new house
to pass the hill of the new
absence
to hear the crumbling
of things -
the same new light
which wrinkles
the clock

to arrive at the same
new place
where children are dancing
for the first   last
time
where leaves are turning
into new graves:
agony
only in agony the world
is moving around

TO REACH THE limb

to raise the voice
    to reach the limb
to turn the clock
    to calm the sleep
to lose the moon
    to glide the dream
to bent the sky
    to cross the beam
to rope the sea
    to gloss the wind
to sleep the heart
    to break the light
to leach the plague
    to dry the song
to lift the hand
    to drop the world

desperately deep and purple

immobile as you are   pure as we could be
exploding in bright colors as we did
feline like the rain we used to sip from
hidden cups
ecstatic -
       ecstatic like a high tide as the
       journey becomes longer and longer
desperately deep and purple and nothing you can
do about -
       sparkling eyes   open mouth
       biting all over like you people of God
       biting and begging for a small piece
       of sky
fluffy   thin as the light
dancing on the ground
       dancing on the hills - too real for this
       day coming so rarely
            to
                  an
                       end:
my memory about to collapse
       dark and cold dark
       and cold I left my little
       pink doll at the end
       of the world
desperately deep and purple and nothing you can
do about
       after centuries
         I am still here
in front of the door

eating earth along with
the stars is now the privilege
of the dead
but a word in my mouth
like a swelling mound still
measures the distance to the
lost sun

*

Angel, for you I am here
in the middle of the shining
wound waiting for my body
to bleed to blossom
to give you new invisible
roots:

*

[a woman is lighter than
your idea about women more
angel than those climbing
your dream   closer to God
than your thoughts about
him   endless like the
earth of her womb moving
like memories under your holy
sleep]

*

I imagine you lost in your own
        emptiness and the wound in my chest
            grows from your never-recovered
                            presence

                    *

                            Earth
to the last dead   air
        to the last flame and then the body
            in its way to God telling new stories
                about nothingness

the day in your hand

moving back and forth
at the pace of the stars:
a marble a beam
a boar or a bone
square like a grave   square
like the falling rain
mostly red   red like a pair
of eyes watching the sun
like tomorrow before dawn
red like the black tie
the early morning funeral
or mostly grey   a hungry mouse
in a grey cage
but colors don't count
don't count at all   the blue
already died
untouched unseen -
move   move again your chair
through the door the smell
of the dead
through your fingers
the yellow liquid moon
the stars
sticking on you   on your blood
flowing all the way to your mouth
to your tongue
what else -
what else could be said
about so little time
about so little space

what I remember

what I remember
about you my green town
fits in one word -
doesn't fit in the whole world -
gardens with watering eyes
lilac-bushes along the sky
and many many windows to open

small days like small figurines
made out of silence and sand -
who broke them all who -
I live now in these long long
sentences   wave after wave
of heavy sounds
is this the first and the very
last language?

and I remember you
people of all kind kneeling
in that small church
on the hill
where I was for ever a child -
what I don't remember is how
I came here to this body
to this name
how I came here
to the last sound

I should say snow

the green turned to black
the black to white
I should say snow -
but the word is like
blood:
doesn't show unless there is
a wound
a wound in the middle of the silence
I should say in the middle of the heart
but the heart just turned
into a sound
a vicious helpless music between
to be and to die

what I learned from a magnolia tree

the pink the white
to open the wings
how to play piano
the sound of the wind
where go the clouds
where is north
where is south
how to bear the silk
of your eyes

successive lives
the snail of time
my shapeless blood
and the shape of the moon
how to rain
how to burn
how to cry
to wear a crown
to build a nest
in my womb

to betray the night
to forget
to close the eyes
to be what I am: the breeze
the frost
the invisible sea:
this is what I learned
from a magnolia tree